# Daily Problems
*and*
# Weekly Puzzlers
# Science

grade
# 3

## by Vicky Shiotsu

**ideal**

# Daily Problems & Weekly Puzzlers
## Science

### GRADE 3

▼▼▼▼▼▼▼▼▼▼▼▼▼▼▼▼▼▼▼▼▼▼▼▼▼▼▼▼▼▼▼▼▼▼▼▼▼▼▼▼▼▼▼▼▼▼▼▼

Vicky Shiotsu was an elementary teacher in Canada for eight years. She now lives in Los Angeles, where she has worked as an editor for an educational publishing company, a tutor to Japanese students, and a teacher at a reading center. She is currently a freelance writer and educational consultant, as well as the mother of two elementary-age school children.

Vicky is the author of over 50 books and other educational materials for students and teachers. These include resource books, bulletin boards, magazine features, textbook materials, and learning games. Vicky's two children share her enthusiasm for science, and the whole family was involved in testing the activities for this book.

Vicky holds a bachelor of education degree from the University of British Columbia, where she also earned her teaching credential.

### ACKNOWLEDGMENTS

Special thanks to teachers Leah and Michael Cole, Ray Adair, and Denton Brazell of Diegueño Country School in Rancho Santa Fe, California, and Carol McKay of Harbor View Elementary School in San Diego, California, for their careful review and student testing of the materials in this book.

Cover Design: Joan K. Takenaka

Cover Illustrations: Ken Bowser

Text Illustrations: Roberta Collier-Morales

Production: Linda Price

Proofreader: Rachel Oberlander

Project Managers: Fran Lesser and Linda Wood

Developed for Ideal School Supply by The Woods Publishing Group, Inc.

Art Director: Nancy Tseng

ISBN: 1-56451-272-X

*Daily Problems and Weekly Puzzlers Science, Grade 3*

© 1998 Ideal School Supply

A Division of Instructional Fair Group, Inc.

A Tribune Education Company

3195 Wilson Drive NW, Grand Rapids, MI 49544 • USA

Duke Street, Wisbech, Cambs, PE13 2AE • UK

# Table of Contents

▼▼▼▼▼▼▼▼▼▼▼▼▼

# Introduction

This book is one in a series of four books for Grades 3 through 6. These books provide a treasury of challenging and engaging problems from all areas of the science curriculum. The Daily Problems and Weekly Puzzlers are each keyed to an appropriate National Science Education (NSE) Standard; many are designed for "hands-on" experiences using common classroom materials.

Students who will enter the work force in the twenty-first century will need to have substantial practice thinking and processing information in different ways. Applying the scientific process in different situations helps students develop useful strategies, techniques, and problem-solving methods that can be used in other areas.

Each book contains 144 Daily Problems and 36 Weekly Puzzlers. The Daily Problems are presented four per page, and most are designed to take 15 minutes or less to solve. The Weekly Puzzlers are more complex, designed to engage students over a longer period of time and to help them develop a variety of science skills. Some Weekly Puzzlers include tips for expanding the activity into a science fair project. Sample answers are provided for the problems, many of which are open-ended or have more than one possible solution.

## Suggestions for Classroom Use

The problems and puzzlers are written for Grade 3, but because the ability levels of students vary greatly, you may want to modify the problems to meet your students' individual needs. For example, you could have your "struggling" students solve portions of whole problems or work with partners. You might require your advanced students to provide more detailed explanations, or to extend the problems and puzzlers in other ways. The emphasis, however, should be on having students come up with creative ideas for solving the problems. The process a student goes through in solving a problem is often more valuable to the student's learning than the actual answer itself.

One NSE Standard and one general subject area are referenced for each of the 144 Daily Problems and 36 Weekly Puzzlers. The chart on page vi indicates which problems and puzzlers are related to each NSE Standard. You can refer to the Standards and subject areas to help you decide how to use the problems and puzzlers. You may want to focus on one Standard or subject area for a week or a month; or you may want to expose students to a variety of Standards and areas over a set period of time. Since many of the problems are related to more than one Standard or subject area, you can use the cross-reference chart as a starting point for choosing the problems and puzzlers you want.

The problems and puzzlers may be given to individual students, pairs of students, or small groups. Working with partners or in small groups gives students an opportunity to share their thinking verbally. Often students are better able to express their thinking in writing after they've had opportunities to express them out loud. Talking about problems with others helps students articulate, clarify, and modify their ideas.

Many of the Weekly Puzzlers and some of the Daily Problems ask students to extend the ideas by applying concepts to new situations and by creating their own problems. When students have the opportunity to apply concepts and create their own problems, they understand ideas more deeply and personally. When they are involved in this way, they are constructing their own meaning as they undertake this creative process.

## Materials

Many of the problems call for the use of materials. We have tried to choose materials commonly found in the classroom or at home. Some of the problems call for the use of basic science equipment, such as magnifying lenses, thermometers, and magnets.

## Hints for Using Problems and Puzzlers

- Use as an early morning warm-up. Put one or more problems on the overhead projector or chalkboard to start your day. Have volunteers explain their answers.
- Give students a Daily Problem or Weekly Puzzler as a daily or weekly homework assignment.
- Have teams work on the same problem during a science-lab period. Then have students take turns explaining answers to the class. Or have groups work on different problems, then rotate the problems when students finish.
- Have an "explanation contest" by seeing who (or which group) can best produce a clear and detailed written explanation of a problem or puzzler with no time limit.
- Use as a transformational activity. Have students turn Daily Problems into Weekly Puzzlers, and Weekly Puzzlers into long-term investigations and explorations.
- Challenge students to create their own problems similar to one or a group of Daily Problems you choose. Compile sets of student-created problems into a quiz for everyone to do. Then correct the quiz as a class so that students can read, answer, and explain their own problems.
- Have students select sample Daily Problems and/or Weekly Puzzlers to put in their portfolios and write about why they chose these problems.

## Getting Started

Work through a few daily and weekly problems with your class before having students work individually or in groups. Encourage students to use their critical thinking, reasoning, and science process skills.

Model both effective and ineffective use of skills when working with your class as a whole. Also model exemplary and incomplete written explanations, as well as productive and unproductive communication in groups. In this way, you will demonstrate and clarify your expectations for students when they are using science skills to solve problems in individual or collective situations.

Show students how to help each other. Emphasize that giving answers to a partner does not help either student understand the concepts involved. You can make a game out of this by having students role-play appropriate and inappropriate ways of interacting with a partner or with a group.

## Wrapping Up

Involve students by discussing the problems as a class after students complete them. Having students share the methods and strategies they use allows all students to develop new skills. During discussions, it is important to emphasize that many problems in science (and life) have multiple solutions. When students see a variety of answers to a problem and hear how other students reached different conclusions, they are more likely to remain open to more than one path or solution.

## Internet Links

The world of science awaits you and your students on the World Wide Web. Listed below are some web sites that may prove useful in the classroom and at home.

The Internet Public Library
www.ipl.org

National Science Teachers Association
www.nsta.org

National Science Foundation
www.nsf.gov

NASA
www.nasa.gov

San Francisco Exploratorium
www.exploratorium.edu

San Diego Zoo
www.sandiegozoo.org

Eisenhower National Clearinghouse for Mathematics and Science Education
www.enc.org

# Cross-Reference Charts

| NSE Standard | Daily Problem Number | Weekly Puzzler Number |
|---|---|---|
| Scientific Processes | 5, 15, 22, 36, 42, 48, 56, 68, 75, 82, 90, 98, 105, 113, 124, 132, 136 | 1, 12, 20, 31 |
| Scientific Thought | 8, 13, 17, 28, 32, 39, 51, 60, 65, 69, 83, 88, 97, 108, 112, 120, 130, 135, 144 | 7, 13, 22, 29, 33 |
| Life Science | 1, 9, 20, 26, 29, 41, 50, 57, 67, 72, 78, 89, 95, 101, 109, 117, 126, 133, 142 | 4, 9, 21, 26 |
| Physical Science | 2, 10, 19, 25, 31, 38, 46, 53, 62, 71, 77, 86, 94, 102, 115, 118, 128, 140, 143 | 2, 15, 18, 28, 35 |
| Earth and Space Science | 3, 14, 23, 33, 40, 45, 54, 63, 76, 80, 92, 96, 106, 116, 119, 127, 134, 141 | 5, 11, 17, 25, 34 |
| Human and Social Science | 4, 12, 18, 24, 30, 37, 47, 55, 61, 70, 79, 85, 99, 103, 110, 122, 125, 137 | 3, 10, 19, 27, 36 |
| Science and Technology | 7, 11, 21, 34, 43, 49, 58, 64, 74, 81, 87, 93, 104, 111, 123, 129, 139 | 6, 16, 24, 32 |
| History and Nature of Science | 6, 16, 27, 35, 44, 52, 59, 66, 73, 84, 91, 100, 107, 114, 121, 131, 138 | 8, 14, 23, 30 |

# Daily Problems

### 1   Growth and Change

Life Science

Think of someone in your class. Imagine that your classmate moves away and you meet that person in five years. List three ways the person's appearance might change. List three ways the person's appearance might stay the same.

*Extra Science Fun!* Get together with one or more friends and look at baby pictures of yourselves. Can you tell who's who? What clues can help you?

### 2   Simple Machines—Rollers

Physical Science

First push a heavy book across your desk with one finger. Next put three pencils under the book. Use your finger to push the book across your desk again. Is it easier or harder to push the book now? What do you think caused the difference in the amount of force you had to use?

### 3   Raindrops and Snowflakes

Earth and Space Science

Raindrops plop but snowflakes float! Why? To help you find out, get two sheets of writing paper. Crumple one into a ball. Hold it in one hand and the flat sheet in the other. Stretch out your arms and drop both objects at the same time. What happens? Why do you think raindrops and snowflakes fall differently?

*Extra Science Fun!* Write a poem describing how raindrops fall. Write another poem describing how snowflakes fall.

### 4   Dental Health

Human and Social Science

You are born with baby teeth that one day fall out and are replaced by permanent teeth. Why is it important to take care of baby teeth if they're not meant to last?

*Extra Science Fun!* Look in a mirror. How many baby teeth do you have? How many permanent teeth do you have?

# Daily Problems

## 5 Experimenting With Sound

Scientific Processes

Jan wants to talk to someone who is across the room. She doesn't want to shout and she doesn't want to walk across the room. What can Jan do to make her voice sound louder?

*Extra Science Fun!* Suppose someone gave Jan a large sheet of paper to help her with her problem. What could she do with the paper to make her voice sound louder?

## 6 Earth and Sun

History and Nature of Science

A very long time ago, a Greek astronomer named Aristarchus said that the Earth moved around the Sun. Most people did not believe him. They thought the Earth stood still while the Sun moved around it. Suppose Aristarchus came back to life and you met him. Write three things you could do to show him that people today believe his ideas about the Earth moving around the Sun.

## 7 Flight

Science and Technology

People have dreamed of flying for thousands of years. At one time, most people thought that a dream like that would never come true. Today, millions of people fly in planes every day. Write about another "dream" that might come true with the help of scientists and inventors.

## 8 Colors and Heat

Scientific Thought

Think about the clothes you wear in summer and in winter. Are summer clothes usually light or dark in color? Are winter clothes usually light or dark in color? Why do you think there is a difference in the colors we wear?

*Extra Science Fun!* Look through catalogs that feature summer and winter clothing. Cut out some of the pictures and make a display showing the differences in the colors of clothing. Do stores feature more dark- or light-colored clothing in summer? What about in winter?

# Daily Problems

## 9  Mystery Bug

Kelly sees a bug in her yard. She doesn't know what kind it is. What could she could do to figure out what the bug is? List four things she should notice about the bug to help her solve the mystery.

## 10  Curved Mirrors

Have you ever thought of using a spoon for a mirror? Get a bright, shiny teaspoon or tablespoon. Then look at your reflection in the bowl (the inside) of the spoon. What do you see? Next, look at your reflection in the back of the spoon. What do you see? What do you think made the difference in the two reflections? Why do you think people use flat mirrors instead of curved mirrors in their bathrooms?

## 11  The Telephone and Communication

Alexander Graham Bell invented the telephone in 1876. Today there are millions of telephones all over the world and more telephone numbers in the United States than anywhere else on Earth! List at least five different reasons for using the phone.

## 12  Sight and Taste

Imagine your parents are preparing blue chicken, green potatoes, and purple peas for dinner. Do you think you would like to try the food? Why or why not? What affects whether or not you want to try a new food?

# Daily Problems

## 13 Pressure and Force

Scientific Thought

Mrs. Lee and her identical twin sister are walking along the beach. Mrs. Lee is wearing three-inch high heels. Her sister is wearing flat sandals. Whose shoes will make deeper marks in the sand. Why?

## 14 Weather and Seasons

Earth and Space Science

Imagine that a friend from another country is planning to visit you. Think about the kinds of weather you have during the year. Write a letter telling your friend what time of year has the best weather for visiting your area. Later, exchange letters with a classmate and compare your choices.

## 15 Breathing Rate

Scientific Processes

You probably know that everybody needs to breathe to live. But do you think everybody breathes at the same rate? Here's one way you can find out. Team up with two or more partners. Then time yourselves for one minute while you count your breaths. (One inhale and one exhale counts as one breath.) Be sure to breathe normally! After a minute, compare your results.

*Extra Science Fun!* What do you think happens to your breathing rate when you exercise hard? What could you do to find out?

## 16 Telling Time

History and Nature of Science

Before there were clocks to measure time, people got up with the sun and went to bed when it got dark. When sundials were invented, people could measure time using the sun's shadow. The first mechanical clocks had only one hand and measured time to the hour. Then, minute hands and second hands were added to measure smaller amounts of time. What do you think would happen if all the clocks and watches in the world disappeared?

# Daily Problems

## 17  Fruit or Vegetable?

Scientific Thought

Lisa is grocery shopping with her mom. "Let's get some vegetables," says Lisa's mom. Then she starts filling her cart with tomatoes, cucumbers, and green peppers. "Wait," says Lisa. "These are fruits, Mom!" Is Lisa right or wrong? Why?

## 18  Skin

Human and Social Science

Do you think the surface of your skin looks the same all over your body? Get a magnifying lens and find out. Look at the front and back of your hands, wrists, arms, legs, and feet. Where does the skin look the smoothest?

## 19  Simple Machines—Levers

Physical Science

Megan gave Kyle a heavy book, a rectangular wooden block, and a sturdy ruler. She challenged Kyle to lift the book without touching it with his hands. After Kyle thought about the problem, he solved it! What did he do?

## 20  Living Things

Life Science

How are you like a dog and tree? Name three ways people, plants, and animals are alike.

# Daily Problems

## 21  Television in the Home

Science and Technology

There's a TV set in almost every home in America. In many homes, those sets are turned on for seven hours each day. Guess how many hours a day your family watches TV. How could you check your guess?

## 22  Flowing Liquids

Scientific Processes

Greg poured some thick syrup onto his pancakes. Then he poured some milk into his glass. What do you think he noticed about the way the syrup poured compared to the way the milk poured?

*Extra Science Fun!* Test two kinds of liquids. Make up a race to see which liquid flows the fastest.

## 23  Seeing Stars

Earth and Space Science

Have you ever looked up at the night sky and seen stars twinkling? Stars seem to "come out" only at night. To find out why, try this activity. Darken the room and shine a flashlight. Can you see the beam of light? Then shine the flashlight in a bright room. What happens? How does this activity help explain why you don't see the stars during the day?

## 24  Different Kinds of Teeth

Human and Social Science

Look in a mirror. Can you see teeth with different shapes? People have four kinds of teeth. See if you can spot them in your mouth:

The front teeth are the *incisors*. They are thin and sharp. Incisors are used for biting. Next to them are the *canines*. They are sharp and pointed. They cut and tear food, especially meat. Next to the canines are the *premolars* and *molars*. They are broad and lumpy. They grind (mash) food to make it easier to swallow.

Think about how you eat an apple. What teeth do you use to bite into the apple? What teeth do you use for chewing the apple? Do you use all your teeth every time you eat?

# Daily Problems

## 25 Musical Glasses

Physical Science

Get two drinking glasses that are exactly the same. Pour some water into one glass. Then pour a different amount of water into the other glass. Tap the sides of the glasses with a pencil. Are the sounds the same? Why do you think that happens?

*Extra Science Fun!* Work with a partner. Fill five or more glasses with different amounts of water. Make up a tune with your glasses. Think of a way to write down the "notes" so that you know which glass to play.

## 26 Animal Defenses—Weapons

Life Science

Have you ever been stung by a bee? Most people probably wish that bees didn't have stingers. But to a bee, a stinger is very important—it is its only way of protecting itself. List five other animals that have special ways of protecting themselves.

## 27 Inventions

History and Nature of Science

List these items in the order you think they were invented: television, computer, telephone, video recorder. At the top of a sheet of paper, write the item you think was invented first and place the one you think was invented last at the bottom of the list. Beside each one, write the date you think it was invented.

## 28 The Force of Air

Scientific Thought

Can you figure out a way to punch a hole in a potato using only a plastic straw? Try it and find out! Get a six-inch length of straw and a raw potato. Then see what happens! (You can use more than one straw if you want to try different ideas.)

# Daily Problems

## 29  How Much Food?

A shrew is a small animal that looks like a mouse. The smallest ones weigh about the same as a penny! Every day the shrew eats its own weight in food—about half an ounce. That may not seem much, but suppose you had to do the same. First weigh yourself. Then get a pound of apples. Figure out how many apples you would need to eat if you had to eat your own weight in food.

## 30  Smell and Taste

Evan has a cold. His nose is stuffed up and food does not taste good to him. To find out why, try this activity with a partner. First blindfold your partner. Then have your partner hold his or her nose and taste one of these juices: apple, orange, or grape. Can your partner name the juice? Why or why not?

## 31  Mirror Images

When Mrs. Boyd came home, she saw a note on the refrigerator from her son Matt. This is what it said: At first, Mrs. Boyd could not read the note. Then she smiled and took it to the bathroom where she was finally able to read the message. How was she able to do that? What did the note say?

*Extra Science Fun!* Write your own message using Matt's method of writing.

## 32  Passing Heat Along

Linda had a cup of hot cocoa. She stirred the cocoa with a metal spoon. Then she got called away. She came back a few minutes later. How do you think the spoon felt when she picked it up? Why?

# Daily Problems

## 33  Wind and Waves

Earth and Space Science

Imagine yourself walking along the beach and looking out at the ocean. There is a light breeze. What do you think the waves look like? Then imagine yourself walking along the same beach during a storm. Do you think the ocean waves will look different? Why?

*Extra Science Fun!* Try this experiment and see if it answers the question. Get a cake pan and fill it half full with water. Hold a straw close to one end of the pan. Use the straw to blow across the water. Blow gently at first, then harder. What happens?

## 34  Uses of Electricity

Science and Technology

Imagine that the electricity went off in your neighborhood for two days. How will your life change during those two days? List as many different ideas as you can.

## 35  A Great Inventor

History and Nature of Science

Thomas Edison invented over 1,000 different things. The light bulb and the record player were two of his inventions. Edison did thousands of experiments. Once, he did 10,000 experiments without getting the answer he wanted. When a friend tried to make him feel better about his failure, Edison said, "I have not failed. I've just found 10,000 ways that won't work." How did Edison feel about experiments that "failed"? Do you think an inventor should give up if his or her ideas don't work right away? Why?

## 36  Air and Work

Scientific Processes

Get a book and a balloon. Put them on a table. Place the balloon's opening over the edge of the table. Then set the book on top of the balloon. Can you figure out a way to lift the book with the help of the balloon?

# Daily Problems

## 37   Catching Colds
Human and Social Science

Have you ever thought of why we say people "catch" colds? People get colds when they breathe in harmful germs. These germs are so tiny that millions of them would fit on a dot the size of the period at the end of this sentence. Germs live in the air and on your skin. Hold your hand over your mouth and cough. Can you feel air rushing out? Think about what happens when a person with a cold coughs or sneezes. What can that person do to keep people nearby from "catching" his or her cold?

## 38   Slopes
Physical Science

Ben has a wagon. Each day he pushes it down the front steps of his house to take it outside. Then he pulls it up the steps to bring it back into the house. One day Ben's father gave him a long board to help him get his wagon in and out of the house more easily. How should Ben use the board?

## 39   Disappearing Water
Scientific Thought

Nicole was doing the dishes. After she washed them, she set them on the dish rack to dry. Before she could get the dish towel, her father asked her to help in the garage. When Nicole came back, the dishes were dry! How did this happen?

## 40   The Spinning Earth
Earth and Space Science

Did you know that the Earth is spinning all the time? It moves around and around, just like a top. Not only that, the Earth spins at 500 miles per hour! Why don't we feel the Earth moving? (Hint: Imagine you are in a large plane that is traveling over 500 miles per hour. You are reading a book. Would you feel as if you were moving at 500 miles per hour?)

# Daily Problems

## 41 Flowers

Flowers are not just pretty to look at—they also have an important job to do! Flowers are the part of the plant that makes the seeds. Without flowers, most plants would eventually die out. In order to make the seeds, though, tiny grains called pollen must be carried from one flower to another. Since flowers don't move, how does that happen?

## 42 Sorting Animals

In this world there are small animals and big animals. There are animals that swim, crawl, fly, or run. Some are furry and some are smooth. Even you are an animal. Make an animal chart. How can you group them? (Hint: Think about land animals, water animals, tame animals, wild animals, number of legs, and so on.)

*Extra Science Fun!* Find out which animal has the most legs.

## 43 Refrigerators

Suppose your family didn't have a refrigerator. How would this change the way your family shops?

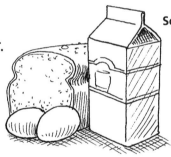

## 44 Fact or Opinion?

Scientists look at the world around them, collect facts, and develop ideas about the world based on those facts. They try to separate scientific ideas from personal beliefs or opinions. Here are some statements about the Earth. Tell whether each statement is a fact or an opinion. Explain your answer.

- Most of the Earth's surface is covered by water.
- Disneyland is the best place in the world.

# Daily Problems

## 45   Sun and Stars

Earth and Space Science

The Sun is a star. Stars are huge balls of glowing gas. When you look up at the sky, stars seem much smaller than the Sun. Yet there are many stars that are much larger than the Sun. Why do you think the Sun looks bigger than the stars? How could you prove your answer?

## 46   The Weight of Air

Physical Science

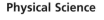

Take a ruler and lay it on a table so that about one-quarter of it sticks out from the edge. Then get a large sheet of newspaper and fold it in half. Lay it over the ruler. Hit the ruler quickly and firmly with your fist—but not too hard. Did you lift the paper easily? Why or why not?

## 47   Handy Fingernails

Human and Social Science

Look at the end of your fingers. Feel your fingernails. How are they different from the rest of the fingers? How do your fingernails help you? (Hint: Think about what it would be like if you didn't have fingernails.)

## 48   Falling Objects

Scientific Processes

Suppose you were holding a sponge ball in one hand and a tennis ball in the other. What would happen if you stood on a chair, held your arms out, and dropped the balls at the same time? Would one object fall faster than the other? Test your idea with objects around the classroom. Use objects that have similar shapes and sizes but different weights. (Examples: long and short pencils; erasers; felt markers)

# Daily Problems

## 49 Telescopes
Science and Technology

Before telescopes were invented, astronomers had only their eyes to look at objects in space. The first telescope was invented in 1608. An Italian scientist named Galileo was the first astronomer to use a telescope. What kinds of things can astronomers do with telescopes that they can't do with only their eyes?

## 50 A Fly's Eyes
Life Science

A fly has eyes so large that they cover most of its head! Each of its two eyes has almost 4,000 lenses that help the fly to see. No two lenses point in the same direction. In comparison, a person has only one lens for each eye. Do you think it would be easier to sneak up on a person or a fly? Why?

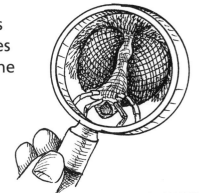

## 51 Water Level
Scientific Thought

Suppose you had a bottle half-full of water. If you tipped the bottle to match the following drawings, how do you think the water would look? Draw a line on each bottle to show where you think the water level would be.

## 52 Studying Animals
History and Nature of Science

A long time ago, scientists studied animals by killing them and collecting them. Today, scientists like to study live animals in the places where they live. Why do you think this is so?

# Daily Problems

## 53 Heat Changes Food

Imagine what it would be like if you had to eat all your food raw! Luckily, we can use heat to cook food. Make a chart to show how heat changes the look and taste of foods. First divide the chart into three columns. Write these headings: *Heat makes food harder. Heat makes food softer. Heat changes the color of food.* Then under each heading, list foods that are changed by heat.

## 54 Temperature

Temperature is a measure of how hot or cold something is. What things can make the outside temperature change each day where you live? What do you think the outside temperature is right now? What is making it that temperature?

## 55 Taking a Breath

You need oxygen to live. You get oxygen by breathing in new air and breathing out used air. When you are resting, you take about 14 breaths a minute. How many breaths is that a day? Do you think you could ever forget to take a breath? Why or why not?

## 56 Air in a Bottle

Get an empty soda bottle. Place it on its side. Then get a small piece of paper and squash it into a pea-sized ball. Put the paper at the edge of the bottle's mouth. What do you think would happen if you blew hard and fast into the bottle's mouth? Try it and see! What happened? Why?

# Daily Problems

## 57 A Desert Plant

Life Science

Have you ever seen a cactus? A cactus has special parts that help it live in the desert. It has long roots that spread out close to the surface of the ground. After a rainfall, the roots collect as much water as possible for the plant. The water is stored in the plant's thick stem. To find out how a thick stem helps a cactus, take two sheets of paper towels and wet them. Roll one sheet up and leave the other flat. Which sheet will dry faster? Why? What would happen if a cactus had a thin stem?

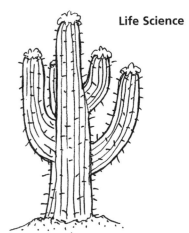

## 58 Photography

Science and Technology

The first photograph was taken in 1826. Before then, people had to paint or draw if they wanted pictures of something. What are some ways people use photographs today?

## 59 Inventions

History and Nature of Science

Inventions have changed the way people live. Do you think inventions make life easier and better? Are there any inventions you wish hadn't been made? Which ones?

## 60 Sunlight and Big Numbers

Scientific Thought

Our Sun is about 93,000,000 miles from Earth. Light travels at about 186,000 miles per second. What if the Sun died out? How long would it take before we knew what had happened? Work with a partner to find the answer. You might want to use a calculator or ask your teacher for help.

# Daily Problems

## 61 Bells and Buzzers

Human and Social Science

If you hear a bell or buzzer at school, what does it mean? If you hear a bell or buzzer at home, what does it mean? What are some other sounds we use to send messages? What do they mean?

## 62 Water From Air

Physical Science

Ashley filled a glass with warm water. She filled another glass with water and ice cubes. She set the glasses on the counter and left them for ten minutes. When she came back, Ashley picked up the glasses. Did the glasses feel wet or dry? Why?

## 63 The Movement of Planets

Earth and Space Science

There are nine planets that travel around the Sun: Mercury, Venus, Earth, Mars, Jupiter, Saturn, Uranus, Neptune, and Pluto. Why don't the planets crash into one another?

## 64 Robots

Science and Technology

Many factories use robots to do certain jobs. These robots don't look like people. They look more like machines. Name three reasons for using robots. Name three reasons for not using robots.

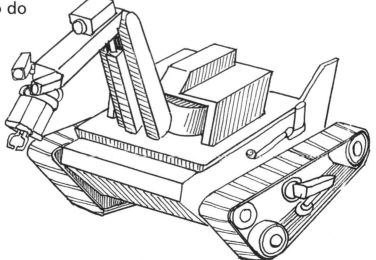

# Daily Problems

## 65  Pressure and Heat

Scientific Thought

Place an ice cube on a paper towel. Then press on the ice cube with a fork for one or two minutes. Remove the fork. Does the ice look different? What do you think happens when you press on the ice?

## 66  Medicine

History and Nature of Science

A very long time ago, a Greek doctor named Galen did experiments on animals. He used the animals to find out more about the human body. Then he wrote books about what he learned. People believed what Galen said. But as time went by, many of his ideas about the human body turned out to be wrong. Why do you think this happened?

## 67  Animal Babies

Life Science

Some animal babies are small copies of their parents. Turtles and lizards fit into this group. Others look very different from their parents at birth. A butterfly, for example, starts out as a caterpillar. Later, it changes into a creature with wings. Decide which of these animals look like their parents when they are born and which ones don't: ant, bee, crab, crocodile, frog, moth, shrimp, snail, snake, whale.

## 68  Onions

Scientific Processes

When you cut an onion, it leaks an oil that turns into a gas. This gas gets into the air and into your eyes and nose. That's what makes you cry. The next time you have to peel and cut an onion, what could you do to keep from crying?

# Daily Problems

## 69   Letting Light Through

**Scientific Thought**

If you hold up a sheet of plastic wrap, you can see through it. We call that *transparent* because most of the light passes through. If you hold up a sheet of wax paper, only some of the light will pass through. We call that *translucent.* A sheet of cardboard won't let any light pass through. We call that *opaque.* Make a list of objects that are transparent, translucent, and opaque.

## 70   Movement

**Human and Social Science**

Do you think you could sit absolutely still for two minutes without any part of your body moving? Why or why not?

## 71   Balance

**Physical Science**

Place a ruler on a table so that part of it sticks out over the edge. Slowly move the ruler farther out over the edge. How far can you move it before it falls? Why do you think the ruler eventually falls over?

*Extra Science Fun!* Do the activity again, but this time set an eraser on the part of the ruler that is resting on the table. Now how far can you move the ruler out over the edge of the table?

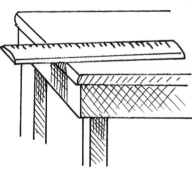

## 72   Seeds

**Life Science**

When you slice an apple in half, you see some seeds inside. Think about all the apples on an apple tree. Think about all the seeds inside all those apples. Do you think every seed will grow into a new tree? Why do apple trees make so many seeds?

# Daily Problems

## 73   Is Science Dangerous?

History and Nature of Science

Scientists sometimes risk their lives to learn something new. Long before airplanes were invented, scientists went up in balloons to learn about the air above the Earth. Can you think of some ways scientists have risked their lives to learn something new?

## 74   Making Inventions Better

Science and Technology

Alexander Graham Bell invented the telephone. But Thomas Edison made it work better. George Eastman made the camera work better. What inventions can you think of that have been made better?

## 75   Water in the Body

Scientific Processes

Did you know that your body is about two-thirds water? That means that if you weigh 60 pounds, about 40 pounds of that weight would be water! Weigh yourself. How many pounds of water are in your body?

## 76   Weather Reports

Earth and Space Science

James Glaisher wrote the first weather report for a newspaper. Look up the weather report in your local newspaper. List five kinds of information you can find.

# Daily Problems

## 77  A Straw Flute

Physical Science

Blow through a plastic straw. Listen to the sound you make. Now cut the straw into pieces of different lengths. Blow through each piece, starting with the longest and ending with the shortest. How does the sound change as the straws get shorter? Why?

## 78  Growing New Body Parts

Life Science

Some animals can grow new body parts to replace those parts that were broken off. Crabs and lobsters can grow new claws. Some lizards can grow new tails. Seastars can grow new legs. People can't grow new body parts, but they can grow body tissues (materials that make up the body parts) to replace those injured or cut off. What are some tissues that can regrow in your body?

## 79  Water Use

Human and Social Science

Did you know that every person in the United States uses about 70 gallons of water a day? List some ways you use water in your home.

## 80  The Sun's Rays

Earth and Space Science

Because the Earth is round, some parts of it get stronger sunlight than others. To show why this happens, get a flashlight and a piece of cardboard. Hold the cardboard upright. Shine the flashlight directly on it. Notice the size and brightness of the circle of light. Now slant the cardboard away from the light. What happens to the circle of light? What part of the Earth

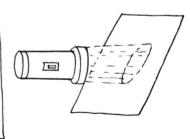

get the strongest sunlight? What part of the Earth gets the weakest sunlight? What do you think strong sunlight does to the Earth? What does weak sunlight do?

# Daily Problems

## 81 Listening to Music

Science and Technology

If you had wanted to listen to music 200 years ago, you would have had to hear it live. Today, you can listen to music almost anywhere and anytime you want. What are some inventions that make that possible?

## 82 Wind

Scientific Processes

We can feel the wind, but we can't see it. When you look out a closed window, what are some ways you can tell if the wind is blowing? How can wind help us? How can wind hurt us?

## 83 Two Puddles

Scientific Thought

It has just stopped raining. Brian goes outside to his yard. He sees two puddles. One puddle is wide and shallow. The other puddle is narrow and deep. The next day Brian goes outside again. He sees that one puddle has disappeared. The other puddle is smaller but is still there. Which puddle has disappeared? Why?

## 84 The Shape of the Earth

History and Nature of Science

When Christopher Columbus sailed across the ocean in 1492, many people thought the Earth was flat. If they went far enough across the ocean, they would fall of the edge. Pretend you are Columbus and you're talking to some sailors. You want them to help you sail your ship across the ocean. They believe the Earth is flat and are afraid to come. What could you say or do to prove the Earth is round?

# Daily Problems

## 85 Clothes and Weather

Human and Social Science

What do you think would happen to your body temperature if you wore a bathing suit in the snow? What would happen to your body temperature if you wore a fur coat on a hot day? Why is it important that we wear clothes that are suitable for the weather?

## 86 Balancing a Seesaw

Physical Science

Suppose you and a friend want to ride a seesaw. If you both weigh the same, where should each of you sit? If one of you is much heavier than the other, where should each of you sit? Use this activity to find the answers.

Cut a cardboard tube in half as shown. Place the flat side down on a table. Balance a ruler across the tube. Put a penny on each end of the ruler. Does it stay balanced? Place another penny on top of one of the pennies. What happens? Slowly slide the stacked pennies toward the middle of the ruler. Can you make the ruler balance?

## 87 Making Work Easier

Science and Technology

Did you know that an American woman came up with the idea for a dishwasher? Sometimes the best ideas for making a job easier come from the people who are doing that job. Think of a job you have to do. What kind of machine would make it easier? Draw a picture of it.

## 88 Ice and Water

Scientific Thought

Sara drew a picture of what she had for lunch. What is wrong with the picture? Hint: Look at the ice cubes.

# Daily Problems

## 89  Amazing Athletes

Imagine this sports event. There are five athletes—a person, a cheetah, a dolphin, a kangaroo, and an elephant. There are five events—running, long jump, weight-lifting, swimming, and discus throw. Every athlete has to do every event. Who do you think will win each event? Who do you think could win the title of *Best All-Around Athlete?*

## 90  Experiments

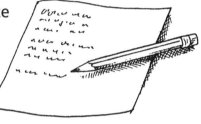

If you did an experiment, what information would you write down so someone else could repeat your experiment? Why do you think it's important for scientists to repeat one another's experiments?

## 91  Scientists at Work

Scientists study the world around them. They study the world to see how it works. They also try to find ways of using the world's resources to make people's lives better. Often, a scientist's work requires patience and great effort. Do you think you would like to be a scientist? Why or why not?

## 92  Clouds

Clouds look solid, but they are actually made up of tiny water droplets! For clouds to form, there needs to be warm air rising. As the air rises, it cools. Do you know what happens next? You can find out with this activity. Put your hand up to your mouth and breathe out. Can you feel your warm breath? Now breathe onto a cool mirror or drinking glass. What do you see? What do you think happens to warm air when it rises high and cools?

# Daily Problems

## 93  Preserving Food

Science and Technology

Think of how food comes packaged to you from the store. Think about how you keep food stored in your home. Some foods can be stored for a long time. Other foods can only be stored for a short time. Make a list of the ways food is stored in your home. Which of these ways keeps the food longest?

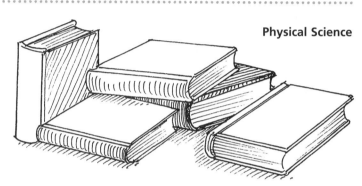

## 94  Carrying a Load

Physical Science

Scott is going to walk to school. He has to carry a heavy load of books. Will it be easier for Scott to carry the books in a backpack or in one hand in a book bag? Why?

## 95  The Skeleton

Life Science

Imagine your body with no bones! Draw a picture of what you think you would look like. Below your picture, write a sentence pointing out one job your skeleton has.

*Extra Science Fun!* Think of an animal that doesn't have a skeleton. Draw a picture of it.

## 96  Space Exploration

Earth and Space Science

Pretend you are planning some space missions to be carried out over the next ten years. Write three questions you hope will be answered by these missions.

# Daily Problems

## 97 Birds

Scientific Thought

Mrs. Lopez and her class were studying birds. She asked her students to tell how birds are different from other animals. Here are the students' suggestions:

- They fly.
- They have feathers.
- They lay eggs.
- They have wings.

Only one sentence tells how birds are different from other animals. Which sentence is it? What is wrong with the other sentences?

---

## 98 Friction

Scientific Processes

Set up a race between a paper clip and an eraser. First place the two objects along the edge of a large book. Then slowly raise the book to see which object will begin moving first. Which object reaches the bottom first and wins the race? Why do you think this happens?

*Extra Science Fun!* Set up a race with other objects. Make a chart showing the results of each race.

---

## 99 Nutrition

Human and Social Science

Fruits and vegetables are good for you. They give you many important vitamins and minerals. If that's true, why wouldn't a glass of grape juice with a plate of apples, pears, lettuce, and tomatoes be a good meal for dinner every night?

*Extra Science Fun!* Write a menu for a nutritious and delicious dinner.

---

## 100 Naming Plants and Animals

History and Nature of Science

A scientist who discovers a new plant or animal species often may name it after himself or herself. For example, a dinosaur called *Baryonyx walkeri* was named after its discoverer, Bill Walker. (*Baryonyx* refers to the dinosaur's heavy claws.) Close your eyes and imagine a new plant or animal. Name the species after yourself. Draw a picture of your discovery.

# Daily Problems

## 101 Animal Defenses—Camouflage

Life Science

Some animals can hide from their enemies because the color of their bodies blends in with their surroundings. This is called *camouflage.*

Think of a place outdoors where an animal could hide. Then draw the animal—it doesn't have to be a real one! Color the animal so that it can use its camouflage to hide in the place you're thinking of.

## 102 Gravity

Physical Science

When an apple falls from a tree, where does it go? If you fall off your bike, where do you go? Gravity pulls on everything and keeps us on the ground. What if suddenly there was no gravity? Name one thing that would be easier to do without gravity. Name one thing that would be harder to do. Even though you can't see gravity, how can you prove it's there?

## 103 Staying Warm

Human and Social Science

If you were an otter or a bird and it was cold outside, you could fluff up your fur or feathers to stay warm. That doesn't work for people. Why? What are three ways people stay warm when it's cold?

## 104 Ships and Wind

Science and Technology

For many years, ships used the wind for power. If a ship sailed near the equator, it had to be very careful of a place called the *doldrums.* There is very little wind in the doldrums. Why would this have been a problem? What about today's ships? Would the doldrums be a problem? Why or why not?

# Daily Problems

## 105    Magnets

Get a magnet and a nail. Do you think you can use a magnet to make other objects into magnets? What could you do to find out? Try out your idea and see what happens.

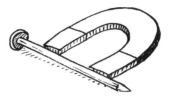

## 106    The Changing Earth

Think about what a new house looks like. Imagine the fresh paint, the new roof, and the yard. Now think about what the house might look like 10 years from now. How will it have changed? What forces in nature will have changed the appearance of the house and the yard? Those forces change the way the Earth looks, too. How is the Earth changing where you live?

## 107    Vaccinations

You've probably had vaccinations (shots) for measles, mumps, and other diseases. The first vaccination was given for smallpox in 1796. Smallpox is a horrible disease that used to kill millions of people. Now, because of vaccinations, people are safe from smallpox. Suppose you had a friend who was afraid of shots. What could you say to help your friend?

## 108    Friction and Work

When you ride your bike, there is friction between the tires and the street. Friction is what slows you down. What would happen if you were riding your bike on a level street and you stopped pedaling? Friction is what causes this to happen.

On an icy sidewalk, would you want more friction or less friction between your shoes and the sidewalk? Why? How could you make more friction or less friction on an icy sidewalk? If you play soccer on slippery grass, would you want more friction or less friction between your shoes and the grass? Why? How could you make more friction or less friction on slippery grass? If you go swimming, do you want more friction or less between your body and the water? Why? How can you make more friction or less friction when you swim?

# Daily Problems

## 109  Plant Parts—Vegetables

Did you know that every time you eat broccoli, you are eating a flower? When you eat asparagus, you eat a stem! Match these different plant parts to the vegetables.

fruit _____

leaf _____

flower _____

seed _____

root _____

lettuce
cucumber
corn
radish
artichoke

See if you can add one more vegetable to each plant part.

## 110  Getting Food

Suppose you had to get some milk, bread, butter, and fresh fruit. Where could you go to get those things? When George Washington was in third grade, where could he have gone to get those things? Which of you could get those things faster? Why?

*Extra Science Fun!* Guess how much time your family spends each week shopping for food. Include the time spent making a list and going to the store. How could you check your guess?

## 111  Color Television

All TV programs used to be shown in black and white. The first color TV program was seen about 50 years ago. Do you think a TV show has to be in color for you to enjoy it? Explain your answer.

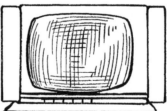

## 112  Humming a Tune

Carolyn asked her dad to hum a tune. Then Carolyn said she could make him stop humming by gently touching him with two fingers. Her dad found that hard to believe but told her to try. What do you think Carolyn did?

# Daily Problems

## 113  The Pulling Power of Magnets

Scientific Processes

Have a partner hold a sheet of paper with a paper clip on it. Move a magnet under the paper. What happens? Try again, using thicker paper. Repeat the activity with other materials such as a book, ruler, wooden board, or glass dish. What did you find out?

*Extra Science Fun!* Predict how many sheets of paper you'd need to stack in order to block the magnet's force. Then test your prediction.

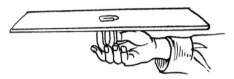

## 114  How Inventions Change

History and the Nature of Science

The first camera was the size of a small room. The first electric dishwasher stood as tall as a person. The first electronic computer filled a whole room. Write a sentence telling how these examples show one way inventions can change over time. How does this change help people?

## 115  Shadows

Physical Science

When you're outside during the day, do you ever look at your shadow? What time of day is your shadow the shortest? What time of day is it the longest? To help answer those questions, try this experiment. Darken a room. Stand a bottle on a table. Hold a flashlight directly over the top of the bottle. Is the shadow of the bottle short or long? Now lower the flashlight and aim it at the side of the bottle. What happens to the shadow of the bottle? Now do you know what time of day your shadow is shortest? What time of day is it longest?

## 116  The Ocean Floor

Earth and Space Science

In some parts of the world, the ocean floor is far below the water's surface. In the deepest part of the ocean, the floor is 6 miles below the surface. Pretend you are over the deepest part of the ocean in a little submarine. If you could make your submarine go straight down from the surface at 60 miles per hour, how long would it take you to touch the ocean floor? Hint: Think about how many minutes there are in an hour. At 60 miles per hour, how far would you go in one minute?

# Daily Problems

## 117  Classifying Animals

Jim had some animal cards. He put them in three rows. The top row had a bear, chimpanzee, whale, and mouse. The middle row had a shark, tuna, salmon, and herring. The bottom row had a penguin, stork, swan, and eagle. In which rows should Jim put the following pictures: bat, ostrich, halibut, flying fish, dolphin, parrot?

*Extra Science Fun!* What is another way you could group the animal cards? List the animals to show how.

## 118  Trapped Air

Waldo the magician is getting ready to perform a magic trick. He needs your help. Everything is ready, but he can't remember how to do the trick. He has a drinking glass with a crumpled up paper towel in the bottom. And he has a tub full of water. He wants to put the glass into the tub and cover it completely with water. But he doesn't want to get the paper towel wet! How can he do that? Tell why it would work. Try it.

## 119  Clouds and Rain

Most people know that rain comes from clouds. Every cloud is made up of tiny water drops. When these drops get big enough, they fall as rain. This happens when the air cools enough for more and more drops to form. Do you think every cloud produces rain? Why or why not?

## 120  Fossils

Dinosaurs made footprints in the ground millions of years ago. Some of those footprints can be seen in rock today. We call them *fossils.* There can be fossils of all sorts of things, even parts of plants. Make a pretend fossil of your own. Flatten some modeling clay. Press a penny into it. Imagine that someone finds your fossil a long time from now. What could that person learn about your penny? Have you ever seen a real fossil? Tell about it.

# Daily Problems

## 121  Careers
History and Nature of Science

Do you ever think about what you will be when you grow up? When your grandparents and great-grandparents were children, they probably didn't think they would become astronauts. That's because there was no such job in those days. Space travel was still a long way off. Now imagine you are going to be a scientist when you grow up. Make up a job you might have that no one has today.

## 122  Your Backbone
Human and Social Science

Feel along the middle of your back and neck. Can you feel the bones that support your back? They make up your backbone, or spine. To find out why your backbone is made up of small bones, get two pipe cleaners and two straws. Thread the pipe cleaner through one straw. Cut the other straw into eight pieces and thread the other pipe cleaner through them. Try bending the pipe cleaners into circles or V-shapes. Which one is easier to bend? What would happen if our spine was made up of one long bone?

## 123  Transportation—Speed
Science and Technology

Suppose you lived in New York City 100 years ago. If you wanted to travel to California, you could go by ship or by train. By ship, the trip took about two months. By train, the trip took about ten days. Today, the trip takes about five hours by plane. What do you think will happen to the ways we travel in the future? Do we need to keep going faster and faster? Why or why not?

## 124  Symmetry
Scientific Processes

If you can fold a shape in half so both sides fit exactly on top of each other, the shape has *symmetry*. Where could you fold this butterfly shape so both sides would fit exactly on top of each other? Draw three more shapes that have symmetry. How could you check for symmetry?

# Daily Problems

## 125  An Unusual Hole

Human and Social Science

Get a cardboard tube (like the one that holds a roll of paper towels). Hold the tube in your right hand and look through it with your right eye. Hold up your left hand in front of your left eye, with palm towards you. What do you see? Why do you think this happens?

## 126  Whales

Life Science

Did you know that a whale is a mammal just like you? Whales are born live and the babies drink their mother's milk. They also breathe with lungs—just like you do. Then how is a whale able to live in the ocean when you can't? What features does it have that help it survive?

## 127  Saving Our Oceans

Earth and Space Science

Craig doesn't like seafood. He doesn't swim and he doesn't care for riding in boats. Do you think he should worry about the oceans being polluted by oil, wastes, chemicals, and other materials? Why?

## 128  Ranking Sounds

Physical Science

There are many kinds of sounds. Some are so soft that you hardly notice them. Others are so loud they hurt your ears. The loudness of sounds is measured in decibels. The higher the decibel, the louder the sound.

| 10 decibels | – | rustling leaves |
| 20 decibels | – | whispering |  acceptable |
| 60 decibels | – | talking |
| 80 decibels | – | heavy traffic |
| 100 decibels | – | jackhammer |  annoying |
| 110 decibels | – | rock music |
| 120 decibels | – | jet airplane |  may damage ears |

Choose six sounds. List them in order from the softest to the loudest.

# Daily Problems

## 129    Thermometer

Press your thumb against the bulb of a thermometer. Keep pressing. What happens to the liquid inside the glass tube? Now put the bulb in cold water. What happens to the liquid in the glass tube? Why do you think this happens? What does a thermometer do? Why do we need thermometers?

## 130    Recycled Air

A gas called *oxygen* is in the air all around us. When you take a breath, the oxygen goes into your lungs. You must have oxygen to live. So do cats and dogs and cows and horses. When you breathe out, your body gives off a gas called *carbon dioxide.* Plants take in carbon dioxide and give off oxygen. Why do you think we never run out of oxygen? What could happen if all the plants in the world disappeared?

## 131    Scientific Knowledge

You know a lot about science. More than you think you do. Write two science questions that you know the answers to. If you asked those questions 500 years ago, could someone answer them? Why or why not?

## 132    Soaps and Detergents

Do you think people really need soaps and detergents for washing off dirt and grease? What kind of experiment could you set up to find out if soaps and detergents make a difference in how clean things get?

# Daily Problems

## 133 Super Ears

Life Science

African elephants have the biggest ears of all animals. They measure up to four feet wide! These elephants can hear a sound two miles away. Would you like to be able to hear like that? Why? Why not?

## 134 Carved By Wind

Earth and Space Science

Wind can pick up sand and blow it against things. What do you think can happen if wind and sand keep blowing against rock for a long time? If you visit Arches National Park in the state of Utah, you can see what has happened. What things do you know of that have been changed by wind and sand?

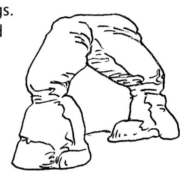

## 135 Objects in Motion

Scientific Thought

Have you ever watched runners in a race? What happens when the runners reach the finish line? Why does this happens?

## 136 Fresh Water and Salt Water

Scientific Processes

Is it easier for a person to float in fresh water or in salt water? To find out, get two glasses. Fill them half full of water. Add four tablespoons of salt to one glass and stir well. Use masking tape. Label one glass *Fresh Water* and the other glass *Salt Water.* Use a spoon to lower a raw egg into the fresh water. What happens? Which type of water would allow you to float better?

*Extra Science Fun!* Here's a fun trick to show your friends. Fill a glass half full with salt water. Very slowly add half a glass of fresh water. Lower an egg into the water. What happens?

# Daily Problems

## 137 Doing Two Things at Once

Pat your head with one hand and pat your stomach with the other hand. Then change the pattern. Rub your head in a circular motion with one hand and rub your stomach in a circular motion with the other hand. Change the pattern again. This time try patting your head with one hand and rubbing your stomach in a circular motion with the other hand. Were any of the activities harder to do than the others? Why?

## 138 Forces of Nature

Have you ever seen an eclipse of the Sun or Moon? Were you afraid? A long time ago, people were frightened by eclipses. What could you have told them so they would not be frightened?

## 139 Making Books

Books, magazines, and newspapers are made by printing presses. What if printing presses had never been invented? How would your life be different?

## 140 Volume

Suppose you had one cup of marbles and one cup of sand. If you emptied both into a two-cup measuring container, would the container be filled to the top? Why or why not?

# Daily Problems

## 141   Space Travel

Earth and Space Science

What if you were chosen to be one of the first astronauts to land on Mars? What is one thing you would like to learn about that planet? What is one fear you might have about landing on Mars? What is one thing you would like to bring back?

## 142   Blue Whales

Life Science

Blue whales are the largest animals on Earth. They can grow to be 100 feet long. How long is that? Guess where 100 feet from where you are right now would be. How could you check your guess?

## 143   Cooling Down

Physical Science

It's a sunny day. Carlos is standing in line for a movie. He is hot and sweaty. The line isn't moving. He is holding a magazine. What could he do with the magazine to make himself more comfortable?

## 144   Force and Movement

Scientific Thought

It takes force to move something. A force can be a push or a pull. Can you always move something by pushing it or pulling it? Why or why not?

# Weekly Puzzlers

## 1   Testing for Fat

Scientific Processes

Think about the last time you ate french fries. What happened when you wiped your hands on a paper napkin? Foods that have fat in them leave greasy spots on paper. Which foods have fat and which foods don't? Here's a simple way to find out.

*Materials:* white sheet of paper, paper towel, pencil, cotton swabs, small amounts of six different foods (examples: peanut butter, margarine, apple, cheese, milk, lemon juice)

1. List the foods on the sheet of paper. Place the sheet on a paper towel.

2. For messy foods, dab a cotton swab with the food item. Make a spot by rubbing the swab gently on the paper beside the name of the food. Foods like an apple slice and a cube of cheese can be picked up and rubbed directly on the paper.

3. Continue making spots on the paper with the other food items.

4. Let the spots dry. Later, check the paper. Star the foods that have fat.

*Science Fair Tip:* Get some packages of food and read the labels. Make a chart showing which foods have fat and which don't.

## 2   Sounds and Vibrations

Physical Science

A sound is made when an object vibrates (moves quickly back and forth). This makes the air around the object vibrate. When the vibrating air reaches our ears, we hear sound.

Put your hand on your throat and speak. Can you feel the vibrations? Look around your home for objects that make sound. Put your hand against each object and see if you can feel any vibrations. List the things you tested. Write whether or not you were able to feel the vibrations.

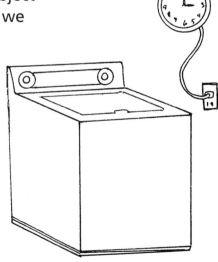

# Weekly Puzzlers

### 3   Recognizing Faces

Human and Social Science

How do you recognize your friends? What is it about their faces that tells you who they are? Here's a fun activity that will tell you something about recognizing people's faces.

Look in magazines or newspapers and clip out two pictures of famous people. Make sure the picture shows a front view of each person's face. Then cut off the top half of one face and the bottom half of the other face. Ask a friend to identify the faces. Which face did your friend find easier to recognize—the one with the top half cut off or the one with the bottom half cut off? Why do you think this happened?

*Science Fair Tip:* Repeat the activity, but ask at least 10 people to identify the pictures. Make a graph showing your results. Write a conclusion about what facial features you think people use to recognize others.

### 4   Animals and Where They Live

Life Science

Think of an animal that lives in the hot, dry desert. Think of an animal that lives where it's snowy and cold. Draw a picture of each animal. Under each picture, write how the animal's body helps it survive in the region where it lives. What would happen if those two animals traded places? Could they survive?

*Extra Science Fun!* Write a paragraph about why humans can live almost anywhere in the world.

# Weekly Puzzlers

## 5 Air Pollution

How clean is the air where you live? Here's one way to find out.

*Materials:* three plastic lids (like the ones from cottage cheese containers), petroleum jelly, masking tape, marking pen, magnifying glass

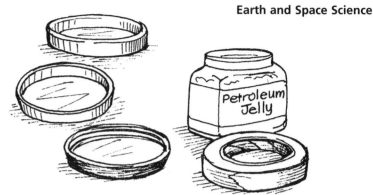

1. Use the masking tape and marking pen to label the lids *1, 2,* and *3.* Spread a thin layer of petroleum jelly inside each lid.

2. Set the lids in three different locations around your home: one outside, one inside, and one by an open window. Tape down the lids if you think they might blow away. Leave the lids for one week.

3. Collect the lids and examine them with a magnifying glass. Write your observations.

Did all the lids look like the same? Which place had the dirtiest air?

## 6 Machines and Work

Machines are designed to help us get our work done and save time. There are very simple machines, like a broom and a dustpan. There are complicated machines, like airplanes and automobiles. Think of all the machines around your house. Choose two. Make up an experiment to show how much time those two machines save.

# Weekly Puzzlers

## 7  How Hard Do Objects Fall?

Scientific Thought

A scientist named Galileo proved that if you drop two objects at the same time, from the same height, they hit the ground at the same time—no matter what they weigh. Suppose you drop a baseball and a tennis ball from the same height at the same time. They will hit the ground together. But do you think they land with the same force? To find the answer, try this experiment.

1. Roll some clay (or play dough) into a large rectangular shape. Make sure the clay is the same thickness all around. Place the clay inside a cookie sheet or metal tray.

2. Hold a small, heavy ball (such as a golf ball) in one hand. Hold a light ball (such as a ping-pong ball) in the other hand. Drop the balls at the same time so that they land on the clay.

3. Study the marks in the clay. Describe what you see.

What does this tell you about the landing force of the two balls?

*Extra Science Fun!* Suppose you wanted to find out if two objects dropped from a greater height land with greater force. Design an experiment using the same materials.

## 8  A Scale for Measuring

History and Nature of Science

Sir Francis Beaufort joined the navy when he was 12 years old. That was more than 200 years ago. While sailing, he watched how the wind blew the ocean water and the sails on his ship. He invented a way to use numbers to tell about the wind and what it was doing. The *Beaufort Scale* is still used today. The scale is numbered from 0 to 12. A 0 means the sea is calm. There is almost no wind. A 10 means very high waves. The sea is white with foam. What do you think a 12 means? Try to find the Beaufort Scale on the Internet.

| Beaufort Number | Description | Observations |
| --- | --- | --- |
| 0 | Calm | Trees don't move; smoke goes straight up; sea calm |

Make up a scale that tells how it rains where you live. When it rains, is it easy to see out the window? How wet do you get outside? Do puddles form? Does the ground get muddy? What else happens? Try to use words like *drizzle, shower,* and *downpour* in your scale.

# Weekly Puzzlers

## 9   Plants and Air

Life Science

Plants need sunlight and water to grow. Do you think they need air, too? Do this experiment to find out.

1. Soak several bean seeds in water overnight.
2. Line the bottom of two bowls with three sheets of paper towels.
3. Put half the bean seeds in one bowl and half the bean seeds in the other.
4. Add water to one bowl so that the seeds are completely covered. Add just enough water in the other bowl to dampen the paper towels.
5. Watch the seeds over several days. Add water as needed to keep the paper towels in the second bowl damp. Record your observations.

What happens to the seeds? Do they look the same or different? What does this tell you about air and plant growth?

*Science Fair Tip:* Make a series of pictures showing how the bean seeds change each day.

## 10   Growth and Proportion

Human and Social Science

Do taller people have longer feet than shorter people? Find out. Take a survey of at least 10 people you know. Use a measuring tape. Measure each person's height. Then trace each person's left foot on a sheet of paper. Be sure the person is wearing socks. Measure the foot from the tip of the longest toe to the tip of the heel. Record your results on a chart. Write a sentence telling what you discovered.

*Extra Science Fun!* Here's a way to display your results. List the names of the 10 people in order of their height. Begin with the shortest people. Then list their names in order of their foot length. Begin with the people who have the shortest feet. Do the two lists match?

# Weekly Puzzlers

## 11  Soil

Pick up a handful of soil. Is it just "dirt"? Here's an activity that might help change the way you look at soil! Use a tall glass jar with a lid. Fill it one-third full with soil. Then fill the jar with water. Screw on the lid. Shake the jar well. Leave the jar for a day.

What do you see inside the jar? Draw a picture of your observations. Is soil made up of more than one material?

*Science Fair Tip:* Get samples of soil from three or four different places. Measure out equal amounts and put them in separate jars. Repeat the activity. Make diagrams comparing the makeup of the soils.

## 12  Shapes and Strength

Here are four shapes made from paper. Which do you think is the strongest? To find out, you'll need four sheets of construction paper, scissors, and tape. Then follow these directions:

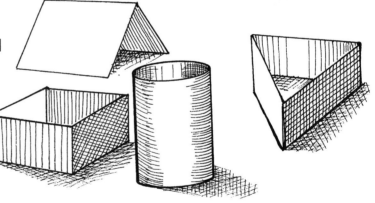

1. Fold one paper in half and stand it on its edges.

2. Roll one paper into a cylinder. Tape the edges together.

3. Fold one paper into thirds. Then make a triangle. Tape the edges together.

4. Fold one paper in half lengthwise. Cut along the fold. Tape the two halves together to make one long strip. Fold the strip into fourths. Tape the edges together to make a square.

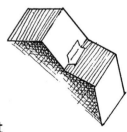

Next test the strength of each shape one shape at a time. Set a light book on top of the shape. Does the shape hold? Keep adding more books until the shape falls apart. Which shape supports the greatest number of books?

# Weekly Puzzlers

## 13  Water and Light

Fill a glass half-way with water. Hold the water up to the light. You'll notice that you can see right through the water because it is *transparent*. Things that are transparent let most of the light shine through. Now think of what you could add to the water to make it *translucent*—that means you can see partly through the water. Some of the light shines through. Next think of what you could add to the water to make it *opaque*—that means you can't see through it at all. It doesn't let any light shine through. Test your ideas and make a chart showing your results.

| I added this to water | Description of water | | |
|---|---|---|---|
| | transparent | translucent | opaque |
| food coloring | ✔ | | |
| a little cornstarch | | ✔ | |

## 14  Observing Animals

Jane Goodall is an English scientist who became well-known for her work with chimpanzees. She studied these animals in Africa for years. In time she won their trust by having daily contact with them. Because of her work, we now know that chimpanzees eat much more than fruits, vegetables, and insects. Goodall discovered that they also eat larger animals, such as pigs and young monkeys. She also observed that chimpanzees use tools.

Goodall, like other scientists who study animals, recorded her observations in a journal. You can, too. Choose an animal in your neighborhood—it can be a pet or a backyard visitor, such as an insect or bird. Study the animal for as long as you can. In your journal describe what the animal looks like, how it moves, what it does, and where it goes. Include a sketch with your observations.

# Weekly Puzzlers

## 15 Bouncing Balls

Do you think that bigger balls bounce higher than smaller balls? Get four or five balls of different sizes. Design an experiment that will help you find the answer. Will you drop the balls from the same height or from different heights? Think about how you will measure how high each bounces.

List the balls on a chart. For each ball, record the height of the first bounce. Write a sentence about what you learned from your experiment.

## 16 Clothing and Fabric

Look at your clothes. What are they made of? Are they made from *natural* fabrics? Or are they made from *synthetic* fabrics? How can you tell? Natural fabrics are made from animals and plants. Wool and cotton are examples of natural fabrics. What are some other natural fabrics? Synthetic fabrics are made from chemicals. Nylon and polyester are examples of synthetic fabrics. What are some other synthetic fabrics?

Make a chart. List the kinds of clothes your family wears and tell what fabrics they are made of. Write a sentence about the kinds of fabrics your family wears.

# Weekly Puzzlers

## 17 Earthquakes

**Earth and Space Science**

Have you ever felt an earthquake? If you have, then you know how it feels when the Earth shakes. The shaking begins deep underground. The ground right above where the shaking starts is called the *epicenter*. That is where the most damage usually happens. To find out why, do this experiment.

Find a large cardboard box whose bottom measures about 12″ × 18″ and six rectangular blocks. Place the box upside down on the floor. Use three blocks to build a "home" near one edge of the box. Simply stand up two blocks and place a third one on top. Build another home at the other end of the box. Then start tapping near one of the homes. What happens? Which home gets the most damage? Why?

## 18 Recognizing Sounds

**Physical Science**

Are sounds easy to recognize? To find out, do this experiment. Find five or six small plastic containers with lids. The containers should all be the same size. Make sure you can't see through them. Put different things in each container. Here are some suggestions: pebbles, coins, nails, marbles, sand, rice. Number each container. Write the numbers on a piece of paper. Beside each number list what you put inside that container.

Ask at least 10 different people to listen while you shake each container. Have them guess what's inside. Keep a record of all the correct guesses. Make a graph to show how many times each sound was correctly recognized.

# Weekly Puzzlers

## 19   Testing Reactions

What does it mean to react? Suppose you're riding your bike down the street and a dog runs right in front of you. How do you react? How fast do you react?

Here's an easy way to test your reaction time. Work with a partner. Have your partner hold a ruler by the upper end, near the 1-inch mark. Put your thumb and forefinger one inch below the ruler. Next, have your partner drop the ruler without warning. Try to catch the ruler as fast as you can. Look to see where your finger caught the ruler. The higher the number, the quicker your reaction time.

Take turns testing your reaction speed several times. Find out if your reaction time gets faster with practice.

## 20   Breaking Up Rocks

Would you be surprised if someone told you that water can break rocks? It may seem impossible. But this experiment will show you how. Use a plastic container with a lid. Fill the container all the way to the top with water. Snap on the lid. Then put the container in the freezer. Leave it there for a day. Later, examine the container. What does it look like? What happened to the water? How did the water change the way the container looked? What do you think happens when water gets into a crack in a rock and freezes?

# Weekly Puzzlers

## 21  Living Under the Ground

Life Science

Many small desert animals, such as insects, lizards, and spiders, live underground during the day. To find out why, do this experiment.

*Materials:* pail, dirt, craft stick, two thermometers

1. Fill a pail with dirt and set it out in the sun for an hour.

2. Feel the dirt near the top of the pail. Dig a hole in the dirt with a stick and feel the dirt near the bottom of the pail.

3. Insert a thermometer into the dirt near the top of the pail. Put the other thermometer into the hole you made. Wait two minutes. Record the temperature on each thermometer.

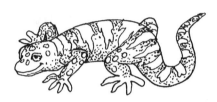

What do you notice about the two temperatures? Why do you think so many desert animals stay underground during the day?

## 22  Water's "Skin"

Scientific Thought

Work with a partner. Use a level surface. Place a penny on a paper towel. Guess how many drops of water will fit on the penny. Write your guess on a piece of paper. Then use an eyedropper to check your guess. Fill the eyedropper with water. Squeeze out one drop at a time onto the coin. Count the drops. As you add each drop, watch how the water on the coin "grows." Keep squeezing the dropper until the water on the coin spills. How close was your guess? Why do you think the water didn't spill sooner than it did?

*Extra Science Fun!* Repeat the activity with other coins. Does your guess get closer to the actual number of drops the more you do the activity?

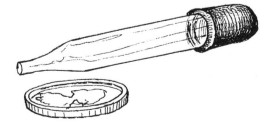

# Weekly Puzzlers

## 23  Inventions and Safety

All cars have windshield wipers. What do windshield wipers do? Did you know that a woman named Mary Anderson invented the first windshield wipers 100 years ago? What would happen if we didn't have windshield wipers?

What other inventions can you name that help keep us safe? Make a picture chart of those inventions. Tell the purpose of each one. Here are some questions to get you thinking: What can you take on a boat to help keep you safe? What do you wear or have on your bike that helps keep you safe? What do you have in your house that helps keep you safe? What about your school?

## 24  Calculators

Why would you want to use a calculator? What can a calculator do that you can't do? Should you be allowed to use a calculator in school? List some reasons for using a calculator in school. List some reasons for not using a calculator in school.

# Weekly Puzzlers

## 25  Warming the Earth

Imagine the Sun shining down on the beach. Which heats faster—the beach or the water? Here's a way to find out.

1. Fill a paper cup half full of sand. Fill another paper cup half-full of water. Measure the temperatures of the sand and the water. Record them on a chart.

2. Place the cups in sunlight for 15 minutes. Measure the temperatures again.

3. Measure the temperature in both cups every 15 minutes for an hour. Record the temperatures on your chart.

Which was hotter at the end of the hour—the sand or the water? What does this tell you about the way the Earth heats up?

## 26  Birdseed Survey

What kinds of seeds do birds like where you live? To find out, get a package with different kinds of birdseed in it. Sort the seeds into the cups of an egg carton. Fill the cups so that there is an equal amount in each. To help you keep track of the seeds you used, number the cups. Then record the numbers on a sheet of paper. Beside each number, tell what kind of seed is in that cup.

Set the seeds outside where birds can get them. Check the seeds once a day. After two or three days, write about what you learned.

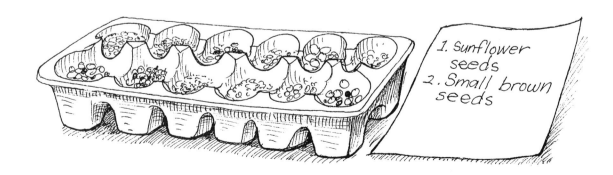

# Weekly Puzzlers

## 27 Body Oil

**Human and Social Science**

Your skin has natural oils in it. What do these oils do? Try this experiment. Fill an eyedropper with water. Squeeze some drops onto the back of your hand. The water should bead up. Now wash your hands with soap and warm water. Dry your hands very well. Now squeeze more drops of water onto the back of your hand. What do you notice? Why do you think this happened? Dry your hand. Rub a little butter or baby oil on it. Squeeze more drops of water onto your hand. What do you notice now? Why does this happen? What can you say about the oils in your skin?

## 28 Separating Colors

**Physical Science**

Use a green felt marker to draw a line on a sheet of paper. The line looks green, doesn't it? Here's an experiment that will show you that colors from a felt marker may not be what they seem.

*Materials:* six washable felt markers of different colors, white paper towel, tall drinking glass

1. Cut the paper towel into six strips about one inch wide. Use one felt marker to draw a wide band about two inches from the bottom of one strip. Do the same thing with each of the other markers.

2. Add about one inch of water to the glass.

3. Place one strip in the glass so that it just touches the water. The end with the band should be at the bottom. Fold the top of the strip over the rim of the glass to keep it from slipping.

4. Watch what happens to the color.

5. Repeat with the other strips.

Write a sentence describing what you observed. How is the color on the strips different from what you expected?

# Weekly Puzzlers

## 29  Inertia

Scientific Thought

Here's a fun "magic" trick you can perform for your friends. It may take a little practice, though.

Get seven pennies. Stack them on a table. Place another penny a few inches to the right or left of the stack. Use your finger to flick the single penny hard, so that it hits the bottom of the stack. If you hit the stack just right, you'll find that the pennies don't fall over. What happens instead? Why? (Hint: Objects at rest—not moving—tend to stay at rest. This property is called *inertia*. Only when force is applied will the object move.)

## 30  Keeping Your Clothes Together

History and Nature of Science

Check what you're wearing. Do your clothes have any buttons or zippers? What do they do? What are some other ways to fasten clothes together? See how many you can list. Collect some of the items on your list. Display them on a chart.

*Science Fair Tip:* Turn your display into a timeline. Tell when each item was invented and make a label telling what it does.

# Weekly Puzzlers

## 31   The Hottest Part of the Day

Scientific Processes

When is it the hottest part of the day? To find out, do this experiment. Hang or tape a thermometer outside. Keep it out of direct sunlight and out of the wind. Check the temperature every hour. Start in the morning and end in the afternoon. Record the times and temperatures on a chart. What did you discover? Make a graph that shows the results of your experiment.

*Science Fair Tip:* Repeat the experiment every day for a week. Make a graph showing the results. Write about what you learned.

## 32   Shapes and Flying

Science and Technology

Why are planes shaped the way they are? People have discovered that certain shapes fly better than others. "Fly" some shapes yourself and you'll find out!

1. You'll need three sheets of paper. Leave the first sheet of paper as it is. Crumple the second sheet into a ball. Use the third one to make a paper airplane. Follow the steps in the diagram below.

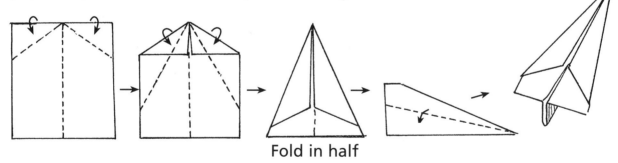

Fold in half

2. Try throwing the first sheet of paper. See how long it stays in the air and how far away it lands.

3. Throw the paper ball. See how long it stays in the air and how far away it lands.

4. Throw the paper airplane. See how long it stays in the air and how far away it lands.

Which shape went the farthest and stayed in the air the longest?

*Extra Science Fun!* Experiment with other paper airplane shapes. See which shape flies the best.

# Weekly Puzzlers

## 33 Oil and Water

Scientific Thought

Can you mix oil and water? Do this experiment to find out. Pour some water into a narrow bottle. Add some blue food coloring. Then add two tablespoons of cooking oil. Put a lid on the bottle and shake it up. What do you notice? Let the bottle sit overnight. What happens to the mixture? Why do you think that happens? What can you say about mixing oil and water?

## 34 Wind and Soil

Earth and Space Science

What happens to bare land when the wind blows across it? Do this experiment to find out. Fill a pan with sand. Place the pan on a sheet of black construction paper. Use a straw to blow across the surface of the sand. What happens?

What happens to land that is covered with plants and trees when the wind blows across it? Do this experiment to find out. Stand some craft sticks up in the sand. Again, use a straw to blow across the surface. What happens? What do you notice? How can plants help protect the land?

# Weekly Puzzlers

### 35  Can You Move Water?

Do you think you can make water move on its own? Here's an experiment to find out. Fill a glass with water. Place the glass next to an empty bowl inside a tub or sink. (Just in case you spill any water.) Now get two paper towels that are connected together. Think of a way to move some of the water out of the glass and into the bowl without using your hands. Hint: You will have to reshape the paper towels.

### 36  Breathing

Take a deep breath. What happens to your chest? Can you feel it expand? To find out how much it expands, do this experiment with a friend. Use a tape measure. Put it under your friend's arms and around the widest part of his or her chest. Record the number of inches around. Now have your friend take a deep breath. Measure again and record the number of inches around. The difference in the two measurements is called chest expansion. How many inches it it? Now have your friend measure you to find your chest expansion.

*Extra Science Fun!* If someone exercises every day or so, do you think that person would have a small chest expansion or a large chest expansion? Tell why.

# Answers

▼▼▼▼▼▼▼▼

## DAILY PROBLEMS

**DP 1:** Possible answers: The person might have grown taller; the face may be longer and less full; the hair style may be different. The color of the person's eyes, skin, and hair; and facial features, such as the shape of the eyes and nose, most likely stayed the same. *Extra Science Fun:* Shape of eyes, nose, and mouth can give clues about who's who.

**DP 2:** It's easier to push the book using the pencils. The pencils allow the book to roll across the desk. It takes less effort (force) to roll an object than it does to slide it across a surface because rolling produces less friction than sliding does.

**DP 3:** The crumpled ball falls quickly; the flat sheet floats to the ground. A snowflake is flatter and has greater surface area than a raindrop; as the snowflake falls, the upward force of the air pushes against its surface, causing it to fall more slowly. *Extra Science Fun:* Poems will vary.

**DP 4:** Baby teeth help prepare the mouth for the permanent teeth that follow; they help the permanent teeth erupt in their "correct" positions. It's important to keep both sets of teeth clean in order to maintain good health, prevent tooth decay, and ward off gum disease. *Extra Science Fun:* Answers will vary.

**DP 5:** Jan can cup her hands around her mouth and talk through them. The "cup" collects the sound waves and sends them forward. *Extra Science Fun:* If Jan rolls the paper into a cone and speaks through the narrow end, her voice will sound louder.

**DP 6:** Possible answers: Show Aristarchus models of the solar system at a planetarium or museum; show him books about space; have an astronomer explain current beliefs about the motion of the Earth around the Sun.

**DP 7:** Answers will vary but might include advancements in space travel, medical research, or environmental studies.

**DP 8:** Summer clothes are usually light-colored; winter clothes are usually dark. Dark surfaces absorb (soak up) more heat than light-colored surfaces. Light-colored clothes help keep you cooler; dark clothes help keep you warmer. *Extra Science Fun:* Stores usually feature lighter colored clothing in summer and darker colored clothing in winter.

**DP 9:** Answers will vary: Kelly could try to find out whether the bug has wings; if it flies; its color; its size; its shape.

**DP 10:** The bowl of the spoon curves down in the middle (concave mirror); if you hold the spoon very close, your reflection is bigger than you, but if you hold it a few inches away, your image is smaller and upside down. The back of the spoon curves up in the middle (convex mirror); your image is smaller and right-side up. A flat mirror gives a more accurate image.

**DP 11:** Possible answers: Call for emergency aid (police, paramedics); make an appointment; chat with a friend; call about business; buy from a catalog.

**DP 12:** Answers will vary. Often, what a food looks like affects what we think it will taste like. Even if a food is delicious, we may not want to try it if it looks strange to us.

**DP 13:** The high heels will make deeper marks. All the pushing force is concentrated into one small area (the heel). Since there is high pressure at that point, the shoes sink deeper. In the sandals, the pressure is more evenly spread out.

**DP 14:** Answers will vary.

**DP 15:** Breathing rates vary among people. *Extra Science Fun:* When you exercise hard, you breathe faster to get extra oxygen into your body. Students could check this by running on the spot for a minute and then finding their breathing rate.

**DP 16:** Answers will vary.

**DP 17:** A botanist (a scientist who studies plants) would agree with Lisa. To a botanist, a fruit is the part of a flowering plant that contains the seeds. In common usage, fruits are generally thought of as the kinds used for desserts and snacks.

**DP 18:** Skin looks different from one part of the body to another, and varies from one person to the next.

**DP 19:** Kyle made a lever with the block and ruler. He slid one end of the ruler under the book. He slid the block under the ruler toward the middle. Then he pushed down on the end of the ruler, lifting up the book.

**DP 20:** Possible answers: They are living things; they grow; they reproduce; they respond to their environment (e.g., changes in temperature); they move in some way (internally or externally); they adapt to changes in their environment.

**DP 21:** Answers will vary. Students can time how long they each watch TV and ask other family members to do the same.

**DP 22:** Possible answer: He noticed that the milk flowed more easily than the syrup, so it poured out faster. *Extra Science Fun:* Students can test common liquids such as water, dishwashing detergent, honey, and molasses.

**DP 23:** The light from the flashlight is easily seen in a darkened room but hard to see in a bright room. Even though stars shine both day and night, they are seen against the night sky but invisible during the day.

**DP 24:** Incisors are used to bite into an apple and premolars/molars are used to chew it. People don't use all their teeth every time they eat.

**DP 25:** When the glass is tapped, the water vibrates and causes the air above it to vibrate. The vibrations reach the ears as sound. The greater the amount of water, the shorter the column of air, and the higher the pitch of the sound. *Extra Science Fun:* Answers will vary.

**DP 26:** Possible answers: lobster—claws; porcupine—quills; rattlesnake—fangs; boar—tusks; owl—talons; rhinoceros—horn.

**DP 27:** Telephone (1876); television (1926); electronic computer (1946); video recorder (1956)

**DP 28:** If the top of the straw is left uncovered, the straw will bend when it's inserted into the potato. If the top of the straw is covered with the thumb, the straw can be forcefully pushed into the potato. The air trapped inside the straw pushes against the inside, keeping the straw from bending—thus making it stronger.

**DP 29:** Answers will vary.

**DP 30:** Answers will vary. The sense of smell affects the sense of taste. When a person is ill, food seems to lose its flavor because it cannot easily be smelled.

**DP 31:** Mrs. Boyd realized the note was a mirror image of the actual message. She held the note up to the bathroom mirror and read: TO MOM   I AM OUT WITH TOM   MATT. *Extra Science Fun:* Answers will vary.

**DP 32:** The spoon was warm. The heat from the hot cocoa was passed on to the cool spoon. Heat moves from a warmer place to a cooler one.

**DP 33:** During a storm, waves are much bigger than when there is only a light breeze. When wind hits the water, it transfers its energy to the surface of the water. This causes the surface water to be pushed upward, forming a wave. The faster a wind moves, the more energy it has, and the bigger (higher) the waves formed. *Extra Science Fun:* Gentle blowing causes small waves. The harder a person blows through the straw, the bigger the waves.

**DP 34:** Possible answers: Might not be able to use the phone; have to wash dishes and clothes by hand; have to use candles or flashlights at night; have to pack food in ice to keep it from spoiling and/or defrosting; might not have heat (or air conditioning); might not be able to cook food.

**DP 35:** Edison didn't get discouraged by experiments that didn't work. He saw his failures as opportunities to learn more about his projects. Answers will vary.

**DP 36:** The book can be lifted up by blowing into the balloon—the air pressure inside the balloon increases and pushes against the book.

**DP 37:** People with colds should cover their mouths when they cough or sneeze. This prevents cold germs from being sprayed out and getting breathed in (caught) by others. People should also wash their hands with soap and water to prevent spreading germs by contact.

**DP 38:** Ben should lean the board against the steps to form a slope. The slope will make it easier to move the wagon up and down the steps.

**DP 39:** The water on the dishes went into the air. As warm air heats water, the water evaporates—it changes into a gas (water vapor).

**DP 40:** People don't feel the Earth move because the movement is so steady and everything else on Earth is moving at the same speed.

**DP 41:** Bees, butterflies, bats, and hummingbirds spread pollen. When they feed on a flower's nectar (a sweet liquid), the pollen grains cling to their bodies and are carried to other flowers. Wind also helps spread pollen.

**DP 42:** Answers will vary. *Extra Science Fun:* the centipede (340 legs)

**DP 43:** Possible answers: You'd need to shop daily for milk, eggs, and other foods that would spoil. You'd have to use frozen foods right away. You would probably use or cook only what you could eat each day.

**DP 44:** *Most of the Earth's surface . . ./ The Earth has more people now . . .* are two facts that can be proven; these statements would be supported by scientists. *Disneyland is . . .* states an opinion.

**DP 45:** Other stars look smaller than the Sun because they are much farther away. Possible answer: Have a tall student walk to one end of the playground; he or she will look shorter because he or she is far away.

**DP 46:** The paper is difficult to lift because the weight of the air is pressing down on it.

**DP 47:** Fingernails are harder than the rest of the fingers. Possible answers: help protect the tips of the fingers; help you peel fruit, pick up small objects, scratch an itch, and scrape away things.

**DP 48:** The balls would land at the same time. Gravity pulls objects to Earth. Objects that have similar shapes and sizes but different weights land together when dropped at the same time from the same height.

**DP 49:** Possible answers: see and study the surface of the moon; observe or discover stars and planets.

**DP 50:** Since a fly can see in almost every direction, it would probably be harder to sneak up on a fly than a person.

**DP 51:**

The surface of the water is always horizontal, no matter which way the container is tipped.

**DP 52:** Today's scientists know that killing an animal will affect the population of that species and that rare species may be destroyed. Scientists don't want to harm animals or change their natural behavior.

**DP 53:** Possible answers: harder—egg, bacon, chicken, bread; softer—rice, macaroni, cheese, carrots; color—meat, shrimp, bread

**DP 54:** Possible answers: time of day, height of the land, cloud cover, time of year, color of the land surface (dark-colored surfaces such as soils absorb more heat than light-colored surfaces). Answers will vary.

**DP 55:** 14 × 60 × 24 = 20, 160 breaths a day. Since breathing is controlled automatically by the brain, a person could not "forget" to take a breath.

**DP 56:** The paper should fly out of the bottle. Blowing into the bottle increases the air pressure (compresses the air) inside. As the pressure equalizes, the compressed air rushes out of the bottle, carrying the paper out with it.

**DP 57:** The flat sheet dries faster. A thick stem helps the cactus store water by making it harder for the water to evaporate. If a cactus had a thin stem, it would lose water quickly.

**DP 58:** Possible answers: record family events; exchange information with those who live far away; enhance magazines, books, and posters; create ads, catalogs, and works of art.

**DP 59:** Answers will vary.

**DP 60:** 93,000,000 ÷ 186,000 = 500 seconds, or about $8\frac{1}{3}$ minutes.

**DP 61:** Possible answers: School—beginning or end of class; fire drill or fire alarm; Home—telephone call; someone at the door; time to wake up; Other—bell to get someone's attention in a shop; clicks to send messages in Morse code; sirens on fire engines, ambulances, and police cars.

**DP 62:** The glass with the warm water feels dry. The one with the ice cubes feels wet where water drops have collected on the outside of the glass. Water vapor in the air condenses (changes from gas to liquid) onto the sides of the cold glass.

**DP 63:** Each planet stays in its own orbit (path) as it moves around its sun because of its initial velocity and the effects of gravitation. The orbits are so far apart that there is no chance of the planets crashing into one another.

**DP 64:** Possible answers: For using robots—they don't get tired; they can work longer hours than people; they don't need to get paid. For not using robots—they may break down or fall apart; they can't learn on their own; they can't handle situations they are not programmed for.

**DP 65:** The ice shows prong marks from the fork. The pressure from the fork produces heat, causing the ice below the prongs to melt.

**DP 66:** Possible answer: Once doctors and scientists were able to cut open dead people, they got a more accurate idea of how the human body works. Galen didn't have the technology we have today that allows us to examine the body closely.

**DP 67:** Animals that look like parents—crocodile, snail, snake, whale; animals that don't—ant, bee, crab, frog, moth, shrimp.

**DP 68:** Possible answer: Peel the onions under water. The water may help keep the oil from escaping into the air.

**DP 69:** Possible answers: transparent—eyeglasses, food containers, windows, soda bottles, jars; translucent—tracing paper, lampshades; opaque—bedroom curtains, wrapping paper.

**DP 70:** Our bodies are constantly moving, either internally or externally. Some movements are voluntary (we have control over those actions), but other movements are involuntary (heart beating, blinking, blood flowing).

**DP 71:** The ruler does not fall off until more than half of it extends beyond the edge of the table. Like all other objects, the ruler has a center of gravity—the point at which it can be balanced. *Extra Science Fun:* Placing an eraser at one end of the ruler shifts the center of gravity, so the ruler can be moved farther out than before.

**DP 72:** Not all seeds grow into plants. Some are eaten by animals. Others land in places where they can't grow. Plants produce many seeds to ensure the survival of their species.

**DP 73:** Answers will vary.

**DP 74:** Answers will vary.

**DP 75:** Answers will vary. Students should multiply their weights by $\frac{2}{3}$ or 0.67 to find out how much of their bodies are water.

**DP 76:** Possible answers: high and low temperatures for the area; weather forecast; comparison of temperatures in different cities; amount of rainfall; phases of the moon; information about tides.

**DP 77:** The sound gets higher as the straws get shorter. Blowing through the straw causes the air inside to vibrate. The shorter the straw (air column), the faster the air vibrates, producing a higher sound.

**DP 78:** Possible answers: skin, hair, nails, bone.

**DP 79:** Possible answers: drinking, cooking, bathing, cleaning objects, watering plants.

**DP 80:** When the light hits the upright cardboard directly, it forms a circle that is slightly brighter near the center; the rays spread out evenly over the area of the circle. When the light hits the slanted cardboard, it forms an oval; the area directly in line with the light is brighter, but the rest of the oval is much dimmer; the rays are spread out over a larger area. The equator gets the strongest sunlight; the poles get the weakest sunlight. Strong sunlight heats the Earth more, causing higher temperatures. Weak sunlight causes lower temperatures.

**DP 81:** Possible answers: radio, record player, tape recorder, compact disc player, television, motion picture projector, video player.

**DP 82:** Possible answers: leaves blow on plants and on the ground; flag waves; someone's hat flies off; hair blows; clouds move; hear wind chimes. Wind can turn windmills that generate electricity; wind cools people when it's warm; wind blows smoke and dirt away. Strong winds can blow down trees and power lines and can damage property; winds can blow fires out of control; winds make it feel colder than it is in winter.

**DP 83:** Possible answer: The wide, shallow puddle is gone; the deep, narrow puddle is still there. Water evaporates (changes to water vapor) from its surface. The larger the surface area, the faster water evaporates.

**DP 84:** Possible answers: Point out that ships sailing beyond the horizon seem to disappear gradually rather than "fall off" quickly. When traveling long distances, some stars seem to disappear and other ones seem to appear. Sail westward and come back to where you started from.

**DP 85:** Body temperature would go down if a person wore a bathing suit in the snow; it would go up if a person wore a fur coat on a hot day. People work the best and feel the most comfortable when body temperature is about 98.6°F wearing suitable clothes helps us keep our body temperature steady.

**DP 86:** The ruler stays balanced with a penny on each end. It becomes unbalanced when another penny is added to one side. It can be balanced again by moving the stacked pennies closer to the middle of the ruler. In the same way, a heavier person should sit closer to the middle of a seesaw to balance the lighter person at the other end.

**DP 87:** Answers will vary.

**DP 88:** Ice is lighter than water. The ice should be floating in the glass.

**DP 89:** Running—cheetah; long jumping—kangaroo; weight-lifting—elephant; swimming—dolphin; discus throwing—person; best all-around athlete—person because only a person can do *all* the events.

**DP 90:** Information should include the theory being tested, the materials needed, the procedure used, observations made, and conclusions drawn. Scientists need to repeat one another's experiments to test ideas; results that can't be verified aren't accepted by other scientists.

**DP 91:** Answers will vary.

**DP 92:** When you breathe onto a cool mirror or window, water vapor in your breath condenses and forms a cloud. When warm air rises, it cools; the water vapor it contains eventually condenses to form the droplets that we see as clouds.

**DP 93:** Possible answers: canned, pickled, frozen, treated with chemicals, wrapped in special packaging materials, placed in plastic containers. Canning keeps food the longest. Once opened, foods treated with chemicals may resist mold and bacteria longer than other foods.

**DP 94:** It will be easier for Scott to carry the books in a backpack. The backpack will spread the weight out over his whole back; it will also help keep Scott evenly balanced.

**DP 95:** The skeleton gives the body its shape. It also protects the soft organs inside. *Extra Science Fun:* Animals that don't have bones include the octopus and the jellyfish.

**DP 96:** Answers will vary.

**DP 97:** Birds are the only animals with feathers. Not all birds can fly; other animals (bats and insects) have wings; other animals (snakes and turtles) lay eggs.

**DP 98:** The paper clip wins the race. It slides more easily because there is less friction between the book and the paper clip than between the book and the eraser. *Extra Science Fun:* Answers will vary.

**DP 99:** The body needs a variety of foods from the different food groups to get all the nutrients it needs for good health.

**DP 100:** Answers will vary.

**DP 101:** Possible answers: A brown snake could hide in a pile of dead leaves; a speckled lizard could hide among pebbles; a green frog could hide on green leaves.

**DP 102:** The apple falls down to the ground. A person falls to the ground. Possible answers: It would be easier to jump high or climb steep stairs; it would be harder to bowl or play soccer because the balls would float. Drop something and watch it fall to the ground.

**DP 103:** The hair on people's bodies is too fine and short to provide much warmth. Possible answers: Put on extra clothing; rub hands together; sip a hot drink; stand near a heater.

**DP 104:** Without wind to push the sails, ships powered by wind could get stranded in the doldrums. Today's ships wouldn't have that problem because they have engines.

**DP 105:** If a nail is rubbed across a magnet at least 30 times in one direction, the nail will become magnetized. It can then pick up paper clips or other small metal

items. Or, you can let the nail hang from the magnet and then pick up items with it.

**DP 106:** Possible changes: peeling paint; outside walls dirty; paved driveway cracked; roof leaking; yard littered with plant matter; soil washed away. Forces of nature—heat of the sun; force of wind; effects of weather (rain, snow, sleet) and freezing.

**DP 107:** Possible answers: The shot will hurt only for awhile; it will keep you from getting a serious disease; if a disease can be wiped out successfully, people won't need protection (vaccinations) against it.

**DP 108:** The bike would slow down and eventually stop. Possible answers: Icy sidewalk—more friction so you don't slip or fall and get hurt; wear shoes or boots with a rough surface; sprinkle sand or salt on the ice. Playing soccer—more friction so you have firm footing when running and kicking the ball. Swimming—less friction so you can swim faster and with less effort; wear a swim cap and oil your body.

**DP 109:** Fruit—cucumber (pumpkin, zucchini); leaf—lettuce (spinach, cabbage); flower—artichoke (cauliflower); seed—corn (peas, kidney beans); root—radish (carrot, beet).

**DP 110:** To a store. When Washington was young, people baked their own bread, milked a cow or bought milk from a dairy farmer, churned butter from milk, and grew their own fruits or bought them from a farmer. It's faster to get those things today because we can buy them all at a grocery store.

**DP 111:** Answers will vary.

**DP 112:** Carolyn gently pinched her dad's nose. People hum by passing air over their vocal cords, which are located in the throat. When Carolyn pinched her dad's nose, she cut off his air supply and he couldn't hum.

**DP 113:** The paper clip moves. Results will vary depending on the strength of the magnet used. *Extra Science Fun:* Answers will vary.

**DP 114:** Inventions can be made smaller. The products are more lightweight, easier to move, and more convenient to store.

**DP 115:** The bottle's shadow is short when the light is shone directly overhead; the shadow gets longer when the light is shone from the side at an angle. Shadows are the shortest during the middle of the day when the Sun is high in the sky. Shadows are longer in the early morning and late afternoon, when the Sun is lower in the sky.

**DP 116:** Since there are 60 minutes in an hour, you go a mile a minute at 60 miles per hour. So it would take 6 minutes to reach the ocean floor.

**DP 117:** Bat—top row (mammals); ostrich—bottom row (birds); halibut and flying fish—middle row (fish); dolphin—top row; parrot—bottom row. *Extra Science Fun:* Possible groupings: water and land animals; flyers and nonflyers; meat eaters, plant eaters, and meat and plant eaters.

**DP 118:** He should push the glass straight down into the water. This traps air inside the glass, preventing water from getting in the glass, thus leaving the paper towel dry.

**DP 119:** Not every cloud produces rain. Water vapor in the air condenses only if the air is cooled enough. If clouds are blown to warmer areas, the water evaporates and the clouds disappear.

**DP 120:** Possible answers: The "fossil" shows the shape and size of the penny; it also gives information about the penny's markings.

**DP 121:** Probably not; rockets powerful enough to leave the earth's gravity and space travel were science fiction until the late 1950s. Answers will vary.

**DP 122:** The pipe cleaner with the eight pieces of straw is easier to bend. If our spines were made up of one long bone, we wouldn't be able to move or bend as well.

**DP 123:** Answers will vary.

**DP 124:** Fold the butterfly along a vertical line through its center. Drawings will vary. Symmetry can be checked by folding along a center line or by placing a mirror along a center line.

**DP 125:** It looks as if there is a hole in the left hand. The right eye and left eye see different things and send two different signals to the brain. The brain combines the images.

**DP 126:** Possible answers: Smooth, rubbery skin and a fish-like shape help a whale move easily through the water. Blubber keeps it warm deep in the sea. A whale can hold its breath a lot longer than people can, but still must come to the surface to breathe.

**DP 127:** Possible reasons to worry about ocean pollution: The ocean is a source of food, electricity, medicine, minerals (such as salt), and jewelry. It affects climate, influences air temperature, and supplies moisture for rain and snow.

**DP 128:** Answers will vary.

**DP 129:** Heat from your hand causes the liquid to expand, so it rises up the tube. Cold water causes the liquid to contract, so it goes down. A thermometer measures temperature (amount of heat). Possible answers: to measure the temperature of the air; to measure body temperature; to measure the temperature inside an oven or a refrigerator.

**DP 130:** Possible answer: We won't run out of oxygen because it is being recycled by plants and animals together. If all the plants in the world disappeared, we would eventually run out of oxygen.

**DP 131:** Answers will vary.

**DP 132:** Possible answer: Wash two soiled materials—one in water and the other in soap and water—and check the results. Soaps and detergents lift grease off surfaces.

**DP 133:** Answers will vary.

**DP 134:** Possible answer: cliffs near a beach

**DP 135:** Runners go beyond the finish line because their inertia keeps them moving. Moving objects tend to keep moving unless a force stops them.

**DP 136:** The egg sinks in fresh water but floats in salt water. Salt water would allow a person to float better. *Extra Science Fun:* The egg floats in the middle of the glass.

**DP 137:** It's harder to pat your head and rub your stomach because your brain has to concentrate more when you want your hands to do two different things at once. With practice, this activity gets easier.

**DP 138:** Possible answer: explain and demonstrate that an eclipses is just a shadow; show how eclipses can be predicted.

**DP 139:** Answers will vary.

**DP 140:** The container would not be filled to the top. The marbles have empty space around them. When the marbles and sand are combined, the sand fills up that space. The marble and sand mixture takes up less space than the separate amounts do.

**DP 141:** Answers will vary.

**DP 142:** A hundred feet is one-third of a football field. Guess can be checked by using a measuring tape.

**DP 143:** Possible answer: He can fan himself with the magazine, speeding up evaporation of the sweat from his skin and bringing in cooler air.

**DP 144:** No; if an object is heavier than the force a person is able to apply, the object will not move. For example, no matter how hard you push on a classroom wall, you won't make it move.

## WEEKLY PUZZLERS

**WP 1:** Answers will vary. Foods such as peanut butter, cheese, and milk contain fat. Most fruits and vegetables contain little or no fat.

**WP 2:** Many items in the home produce a steady sound and vibrations: washing machine, electric clock, radio, television, computer.

**WP 3:** In general, the face with the bottom half cut off is easier to recognize because most people use hair, eyes, and eyebrows to recognize faces. The picture without those features is harder to recognize.

**WP 4:** Possible answers: Desert animals have bodies that help them lose heat and stay cool. Some are able to go for long periods without water. Polar animals have furry bodies and layers of fat that that help them withstand freezing temperatures. *Extra Science Fun:* People are able to live anywhere because they can make clothing and shelters suited to different environments.

**WP 5:** Results will vary. The lid with the most particles indicates the place that had the dirtiest air.

**WP 6:** Possible answers: Time how long it takes to do a job by hand, then time how long it takes to do the job with a machine. Or time two people doing the same job, where only one uses a tool or a machine. Examples: whipping butter into cream using a spoon and using an egg-beater; cracking nuts by banging them against a table and by using a nutcracker; sewing two pieces of cloth together by hand and with a sewing machine.

**WP 7:** The heavier ball lands with greater force, leaving a deeper mark in the clay. To see if height affects the force with which an object lands, the balls could be dropped from different heights and then the marks left in the clay could be examined. Objects dropped from greater heights make deeper marks, indicating greater force.

**WP 8:** Possible answer: A 12 means hurricane winds and extremely high waves. Answers will vary.

**WP 9:** The bean seeds in both bowls sprout. The ones underwater stop growing after a few days because they don't have enough air to continue growing.

**WP 10:** Generally, taller people have longer feet than shorter people do.

**WP 11:** The soil separates into layers. The heavier materials settle in layers on the bottom of the jar according to their densities. Lighter materials such as humus—dead matter that provides nutrients in the soil—float near the top. Different kinds of soils have varying amounts of materials such as sand, silt, clay, gravel, and humus.

**WP 12:** The cylinder is the strongest. It can hold more books because their weight is more evenly spread out over it.

**WP 13:** Examples: Food coloring keeps the water transparent; a little bit of cornstarch makes the water translucent; a lot of cornstarch makes the water opaque.

**WP 14:** Observations will vary.

**WP 15:** Possible answer: Drop the balls from the same height in front of a sheet of butcher paper and then mark on the paper how high the ball bounces. Bigger balls do not necessarily bounce higher. The material that the balls are made from affects the way they bounce.

**WP 16:** Other natural fabrics—linen, silk, animal fur; other synthetic fabrics—rayon, acetate, acrylic, spandex. Answers will vary.

**WP 17:** Tapping the box sends out waves of energy that weaken as they move outward. The "home" nearer the source of the tapping is damaged more because it received more energy. In the same way, an earthquake sends out waves of energy that weaken as they move farther away from the epicenter.

**WP 18:** Results will vary.

**WP 19:** To react means to assess a situation, decide what to do, and take action. Possible answer: Put on the brakes or steer around the dog as quickly as possible to avoid an accident. Reaction time should get faster with practice; the more someone practices a response, the faster and more smoothly the brain, nerves, and muscles are able to carry out the action.

**WP 20:** As the water in the container freezes, it expands. It may push out the sides of the container or force the lid off. When water seeps into cracks in rocks and freezes, the pushing force of the ice sometimes splits rocks apart.

**WP 21:** The temperature near the top of the pail will be greater than the temperature near the bottom. Many desert animals stay underground because it's cooler.

**WP 22:** As the drops fall on the coin, the water bulges. The surface tension of the water keeps the drops together, forming a thin "skin." When there is too much water for the "skin" to hold, the water spills.

**WP 23:** Windshield wipers wipe rain or snow off the window of a vehicle. Without them, it would be hard to see and dangerous to drive in rain or snow.

Possible answers: Boat—life jackets and life preservers; Bike—horn or buzzer and reflectors; wearing a helmet; House—smoke detectors, burglar alarm, circuit breakers, fire extinguishers; School—fire extinguishers, sprinkler system, smoke detectors, fire exits, fire doors.

**WP 24:** Possible answers: Calculators can perform complex math operations quickly, especially when working with large numbers. Calculators can be used to perform operations that students haven't learned yet. Answers will vary.

**WP 25:** The soil and the water measure the same temperature at the beginning of the experiment. At the end of an hour, the soil is warmer than the water. When the Sun warms the Earth, the land heats up more quickly than the water.

**WP 26:** Results will vary.

**WP 27:** After hands are washed with soap and water, the drops spread out (don't bead up) because the natural oils have been washed away. After rubbing on a little butter or baby oil, the water beads up again because oil was added back. The oils in skin repel water and cause it to form beads.

**WP 28:** All the strips will show bands of color stretched out along the paper. Some of the colors will have separated into two or more colors. (Example: Green may separate into yellow, green, and blue.)

**WP 29:** The bottom penny shoots out. The rest of the stack remains intact because the force of the moving penny was focused on only the bottom coin. The inertia of the other coins keeps them in the stack.

**WP 30:** Buttons and zippers help keep clothes on. Other fasteners—hook-and-eye, snaps, laces, Velcro.

**WP 31:** The temperatures are the highest during the middle of the afternoon.

**WP 32:** The paper plane flies farther than the sheet of paper and the paper ball.

**WP 33:** After shaking, the droplets of oil are spread throughout the water. After standing overnight, the liquids separate, with the oil floating on top of the water. Oil is lighter (less dense) than water. Oil and water do not stayed mixed.

**WP 34:** When you blow across the sand, a lot of the sand is blown out of the pan. Less sand is blown away when the craft sticks are placed in it. Plants help reduce the amount of surface erosion that takes place as a result of wind action.

**WP 35:** Possible answer: Make a "rope" by twisting the paper towels tightly together. Then place one end of the "rope" in the glass and the other end in the bowl. The paper towel has millions of tiny spaces between its fibers. The water moves into these spaces and eventually will drip into the bowl.

**WP 36:** Results will vary, but students should notice that their chests get a little larger when they take a deep breath. *Extra Science Fun:* A person who exercises regularly should have a slightly larger chest expansion that one who does not.